I still REMEMBER the NAMES of YOUR DEMONS

MELANIE STROHMAIER

I Still Remember The Names Of Your Demons
© 2021 Melanie Strohmaier

Siedlerweg 14
83088 Kiefersfelden
Deutschland

melanie@strohmaier.com.de

Cover & Photography: © Melanie Strohmaier
Layout: © Melanie Strohmaier
Illustrations: Melanie Strohmaier
Illustration 'Rose': Mel Engisch
Proofreading: Nicole Sachs

KDP-**ISBN:** 9798463553577
Imprint: Independently published

First Edition
via Kindle Direct Publishing
Printed and bound: Amazon KDP

Bibliografische Information der Deutschen Nationalbibliothek:
Die Deutsche Nationalbibliothek verzeichnet diese Publikation in der Deutschen Nationalbibliografie; detaillierte bibliografische Daten sind im Internet über http://dnb.dnb.de abrufbar.

FOR THE STRANGER WHO BROKE ME INTO ONE MILLION PIECES
WITHOUT EVER TOUCHING ME

~ silence is the most powerful sword

I.

I WANT TO WRITE ABOUT THE SCARS PEOPLE LEAVE BEHIND.

I create whole worlds out of nightmares.
I write poems about the scent of the night. About the stars and
why I see them differently since you started to forget me.
I want to hide secrets between the lines and hide truths as secrets. I
write about people I never really met but in my dreams. About
touches that go deeper than skin and connections that break as
easily as snowflakes in the wind.

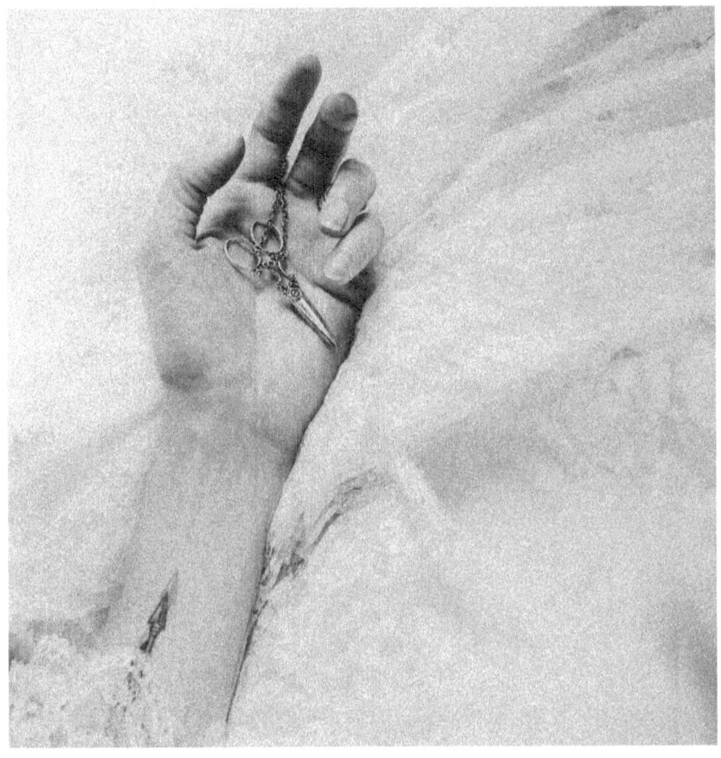

TIME

Time was never on our side. A false hope, that flared up in us – *dangerous* – like a drop of oil in fire. *Growing up is worse than I thought.* I wish for the time back, when the days were a small eternity, blithe and as light as the transparent wings of a dragonfly. When you are young, you're convinced that nothing and no one can harm you. The world would lie ahead, *waiting just for you* and the days would never end. Even the summers were full of magic – *infinite* – days stretched like thick honey. A fingertip full of it was enough to forget everything around you. The heavy sweetness on our lips was all we needed. Until we wake up from our dream and notice that each day is going by faster than the previous one. *Time has a strange consistency.* It changes its texture like the clouds in the sky change their shape. And with each passing year, we feel the lost time like merciless kisses from nightshade. *And now* ... the taste of honey on our tongues is just a distant memory that continues to fade.

MARKS

We leave marks on all the things we touch and lose. Fingerprints that can never be washed off. No matter where we go – *we never go forever.*

.

You hide the marks on your skin with such delicate ease and artistic perfection that I can't help, but never say a word. I pretend not to notice your scars and I smile, while I just want to hold you and take away all your pain. You draw your scars with the dedication of an artist, who paints his art only for himself. Hidden masterpieces of dark memories. Every wound tells a story – every scar proves your strength. You are still here and fight with the brightest colors against your inner demons. *Crimson red is your favorite.* I wish I would know what broke you so bad. What kind of demons made you such an obsessive creator of self-destructive art?

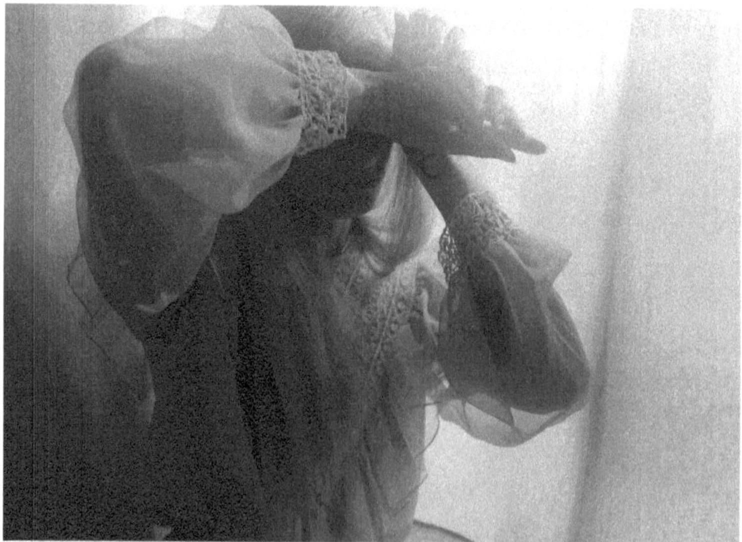

KISS

You will forget me with each of her kisses.

And I'll vanish into a hidden corner of your memories – *slowly fading* – until I'm nothing more than the hint of a feeling. A longing in your heart that you can't decode anymore. You were always far away and close at the same time. I smile but my lungs are slowly filling with blood – *I don't mind choking.*

Would you just kiss me once and then never again?

I'd love to know how your lips taste on a cold winter night.

ALONE

The silence here in my room is louder than my thoughts. I can't remember when I lost myself at the sight of the misty mountains. All that gray and white dust is filling my mind like a noiseless lullaby. The clock is ticking second by second – *time seems endless far away* – like ages that pass, while I have the memory of a name on my lips. I feel hypnotized and my heart aches for something that I can never have. All my thoughts fade with every tick. At the end oft he day, all that's left within me is a silence and an emptiness that could swallow whole worlds.

And I wonder if I am alone or just missing someone that I've never felt.

DEMONS

My first mistake was to let them into my life to haunt me.
To not fight them when they tried to take everything away from
me. Many years I was too weak to call them by their names.
Instead, I ran away breathlessly and hid myself under my blankets
like a child. *Not even the lights could kill you.*

My second mistake was trying to kill my demons.
I felt strong enough to fight back. But they defeated me with my
own weapons. I can't remember when they found me, or why it
was me they wanted. Out of the darkness, nightmares were born.
And I don't know which night was so abysmally black that it
created you. You're a child of the dark – ruler of the shadows. *But I
started to fall for you, like I always fell for certain darkness.*

My third mistake was exactly that – *falling.*
I let every feeling go, pushed it away and became my own ghost.
Numb, emotionless and ice-cold. Until I'd found true weapons
against you. I made friends with all my fears, wore my melancholy
like a black evening dress. *The blackest you'll ever see.* My lips are
crimson from my own blood because I know how much you desire
the taste. This time, the dagger won't be made of silver – but three
words that will bring you to your knees.

Do you want to have this last dance with me tonight?

SECRETS

When we talk, I love to listen to your voice like to my favorite song
— *I could listen to it for hours.* You have the gift to tell things with such
a deep passion that I can't but admire you with all my heart. You
describe what you see and feel with a poetical clarity, like a writer,
who is not aware of his own magic. Conversations with you are like
an addictive story that I hope will never find an end. But slowly, I
feel the change in us that time creates silently and without mercy.
You start to hide words between the lines — *paint over them with
metaphors of silence.* And I do the same because the words lie so
heavy on my tongue that I taste blood. I know you would choke if
I'd speak them out loud. And you'd rather bite your lips than kiss
the words from my mine.

Some things are meant to stay secrets.

But I think what we hide …
… is the same.

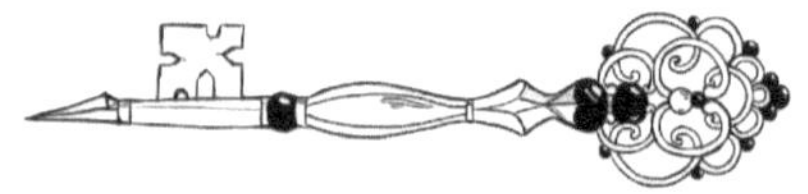

BLUE

The noise around me is deafening and with all my strength, I have to concentrate not to lose myself somewhere

— In words of strangers, in loud laughter. In bright lights and questions that are not addressed to me. In a world, no one else sees. The shadows have always had an eerie attraction to me. The warmth increases — the heat makes my cheeks glow — yet I hide my trembling hands in the pockets of my coat. Music rushes in the background, *distorted,* almost like distant waves. I listen, *blink,* get my thoughts straight again. *How long will I hold out this time?* Although my head feels empty as if someone has just left rubble and ashes — a name keeps pushing into my memory. And while all the noises merge into one, I finally sink into the whirring that slowly turns into a whisper. A longing that comes from the depths of my heart. Even though the feeling will never drown out the noise, I can hear it as clearly as the thunder on the horizon.

Your eyes have a color of blue I've never seen before. And I wonder how the shade would change on a cold autumn morning, when you face me for the very first time. Maybe I'd give them the most beautiful name.

.

II. I love the way the blue of your eyes turns into shades of emerald when dusk kisses you in the forest.

Every time I see your colors my mind creates new words for it. I am an artist who tries to find the most beautiful colors to paint your mind.

ROSE

Dreaming of you
is the same feeling
as kissing thorns
with a devoted
self-destruction

Metal doesn't taste much different than blood

"Red as blood"
I sing with the smile
of a liar whispering
as if drunken from
the heavy smell
of a field full of
buried secrets

Oh, and all that beauty will turn to ash

And I think
that is the reason
why red roses
have the meaning
of true love

I've always been the kind of girl who preferred wildflowers

NEON

The neon lights burn my eyes with pink and blue fires.
But I've never seen anything more beautiful than your face in the colors of the city at night.

The city is quiet as I drown in the sound of your voice.

You stop in front of a huge shop window. Your shadows are painted in neon blue and as I try to see what you see behind the glass, your reflection starts to smile.

"Blue is my favorite color," I whisper, as you get closer, still staring at your dreamlike reflection.

"What do you see?" you ask curiously.

"Only us," I lie and think *and the empty streets at midnight, but our reflections seem distorted, as if there's a completely different world beyond the glass. And we're totally different people. Maybe he's someone who could love me.* "Why did you smile?" I ask instead, hiding my secret carefully.

You light a cigarette and the smell of smoke hits me with a deep nostalgia.

"Because I remembered something," you reply.

I turn my head – I want to see the real version of you, not just your reflection. The smoke around you glows like some kind of radioactive mist. *I knew you in another world,* I think but no sound leaves my lips.

You watch me thoughtfully but decisively – look deep into my eyes, through me at first. Then, after seconds, you seem to get clear, and your eyes reach my soul and my heart.

And while you speak, our connection pulls so heavy on my soul, that it feels like we'd collide at any moment.

"I remembered that I've fallen for neon blue since the day I first met you in my dreams," you answer. "You never told me your name, but I immediately recognized you in this world."

I shiver and feel such a desperate longing inside that I can't even breathe. *The only thing I want is your lips on mine.*

Before I can answer, you put your arms around me and hold me tight.

"And even if this world dies too, I'll find you in the next. I will burn everything down to find you ..."

Your words calm the fear in me as if they were a lullaby that you sing just for me. And as I lay my cheek against your chest, I close my eyes.

But the neon lights don't disappear.

"I've asked you that before, haven't I?"

A spark flamed up in his eyes, as if he painfully remembered something but couldn't hold the pictures in his mind. "Somehow I can't remember."

"Yes, you have," she whispered, trying not to lose control over her feelings. The wind was icy, and she sank deeper into the warm woolen scarf that was wrapped around her neck. "It's okay ... But I remember something about you," she said instead, maybe to calm his confused mind. "You always told me how much you love this stormy and freezing cold weather."

I'll never forget the glow in your eyes when the first snow fell.

His gaze wandered from her to the sky, slowly getting lost in the slate gray. "Why did I ask you that before, but can't remember the answer ...?" It seemed as if he was more talking to himself than to her. "Why the hell do you know things about me and I ...," he stopped angrily, *torn inside.* "... feel like I'm stuck in some weird daydream?"

She smiled, but inside she died a million deaths. "I will tell you the answers to your questions as often as necessary," she assured to him. "They took all your memories, but they can never take away your feelings ..." Her voice broke.

He stood there, silently watching the clouds rush by, *but something changed,* as he listened to her voice. "Maybe you're right ..."

The first snowflakes fell from the sky, thick like dandelions. He took a step closer to her, touched a snowflake that landed on her cheek. "Your name ..." he started softly, "... was the same as the flower's, I fell in love with last summer."

You're right. But even if you fell in love with the flower, your true love will always be winter, she thought.

MOONSTRUCK

I've always heard someone calling for me
when I looked at the moon
like a spark of magic whispering my name
no matter how far away you are
hours, centuries, worlds
I've always heard your call
I felt your longing, your heartbeat
and I waited for you to find me
in every night, in every dream, in every nightmare

But now I'm the only one who's drowning
in memories and sadness and distance
that have never been further away

There's stardust running through my veins

But tonight, the air is filled with silence
because you fell in love with daylight

WORDS

I always try to find the most exquisite words
to describe you or the feeling you leave
inside of my soul, in the depths of my heart
but I slowly have used up my vocabulary
and no poem seems ever good enough

No words – no matter how deep or how beautiful or how cruel
can describe the pain of how it feels like to be forgotten by you
and the worlds splintered, as you took their nights with you
because you don't fear them any longer

No sentence or lullaby or thousand pages
can express the emptiness you left in my bones
I carve your name in ivory white
while I sing with the voice of a drowning soul
but you never answered my silent question

Your lips remain silent, *just like your fingertips*

AUTUMN

I forgot how much I love the smell of cold air
– a hint of smoke and sweet decay

I stare at the sky for a few moments too long,
looking for the half-forgotten dream I had.
The sun breaks through anthracite clouds
– flowing around branches in ribbons of liquid gold

Last autumn I lost something to someone

My fingers go numb, I can barely write this down.
I feel the remnants of a feeling in the wind
– touches my skin like a broken promise
And for the first time, I don't feel like I'm drowning ...

... while I whisper a silent goodbye.

ROOF

I wander through this city like a ghost.

I've never been here before — *an unwelcome sleepwalker in someone else's dream.* You still have the key to this world, so I have no idea how I got here. It's incredibly dark, only the crescent moon sends its sickly-looking rays through the narrow gaps of the skyscrapers — *huge monsters made of concrete and glass and coldness.*
   Suddenly
         — a breath —
               — a blink —
                       — dream-seconds later —
I climb the rusty-red steps of an abandoned factory, until I step through a nonexistent door. The gloomy neon sky welcomes me with an icy kiss. I wish you would be here with nothing between us — not even air between our lips. Too close to breathe.
   But close enough to forget we're from different worlds.
   My steps echo unnaturally loud in the quiet of the night. Stones, dust and pieces of metal crunch under the soles of my boots — *crumbled relics of bygone times. Leftovers from an intact world.* Moonlight shadows on the concrete floor — flowing and angular at the same time.
         — Crack in reality —
               — split-second —
                     — breath —
As I open my eyes, you're standing in front of me, at the edge of the roof. *Breaking heartbeat.* You're looking over the city that is more yours than reality ever was. But only I know, you're also just a visitor to this dream.
         — Heartbeat —
               — rushing memories —
                     — hurricane —
  I smile because I know how this dream ends.
      Every.
            Time.
                  Again.

HIRAETH

First: I can't remember when this longing in my chest began. It started as a whisper – gentle waves that soaked my heart with salty-sweet questions. I never cared about the answers. But things change, *as they always do. They grow and give and take at the same time.*
Second: The desire slowly became a roaring monster – screaming for something that is forever out of reach. *It always knew, but never stopped anyway.* I wanted answers, even if I've already forgotten the questions.
Third: The monster fell asleep again – changed into something different. A blank space that nothing and no one could ever fill. The void feels like the empty pages in a book (*that a stranger is holding in his hands – not able to read.*)
Fourth: *Feelings overflow, and I can't stop them.* I want to run towards you – *collide* – wrap my arms around you and hold you close. I want to know how you feel – *how your skin feels on mine.* How your closeness burns my coldness. *And I know my demons would fall silent for the first time. Because you are the only one who knows their names.*

O n some days ...
... I feel this urgent need – a desire that is so deep that it tears me apart from the inside out. And no matter where you are or how many worlds lie between us, I'll never stop searching. I want to run towards you – *collide* – wrap my arms around you and hold you close. I want to know how you feel – *how your skin feels on mine*. How your closeness burns my coldness. And I don't know why but I would feel like a whole for the first time in my life.

Because I would never get closer to the missing part of my soul than with your arms around me and our hearts beating in the same rhythm. Maybe my broken melody would sing in the right notes again.

Now I feel like the empty pages in a book, that a stranger is holding in his hands – *not able to read*.

Do you sometimes wonder, who's the writer of your blank book?

BONES

*S*how me your bruises.

I'd love to find out if we have scars in the same shapes. Constellations of the past that follow us everywhere we go. *Blue and crimson and purple.* Silver lines on our skin that hurt when the weather changes. A merciless reminder that demons don't live just in our dreams. *Some are human too.*

Show me your pain.

Tell me everything that ever hurt you. Broken bones can never be more painful than the screams of the demons that haunt you in your dreams. *Whisper every secret to me, every fear that eats you up from the inside.* Shadows under tired eyes – emptiness can be a color too. *I would name it shadowpaintersdisease.*

Show me your deepest desires.

I want to know what you long for – your dreams and the things you love. The details you see that other people don't. The feelings you get when you watch the stars. The words that come to your mind when you remember your dearest memories. The longing that burns deep inside of your bones.

And I smile as I listen to your secrets but never utter mine.

"Now the time has come, my old friend ..." the girl whispered, lovely, almost singing.

The monster was still hiding like a dangerous predator – *lurking and waiting for the right moment. Did you miss me?*, asked the familiar voice seductively in her head – took everything away, suppressed any doubt. *You know this is your end. I don't fear a little girl who has forgotten her own name centuries ago.*

The girl leaned further down, humming a tune, as if she tried to sing the monster to sleep. *Her heart a music box, irreparably broken in her chest.* She smiled and her beauty made even the monster tremble. "I may have lost my name in a stranger's dream long time ago,

but my dear ..."

Now the monster flew around her like a swarm of black bees – *noiselessly.* Kissed her with desire, touched her with shadows, buried her in the dark. *Took every memory.*

But she felt no pain, as the last words left her lips like a breath of wind.

"*... I still remember yours.*"

INCOMPLETE

I've always cried with words instead of tears. Maybe that's why so many poems have flowed out of my heart lately. I feel incomplete without these nights, and I don't know how many metaphors I can find to describe how much I miss you.

Could you please give me back what you took with you?

NOSTALGIA

I still remember how summer felt as a child.

What it was like to run through a thunderstorm without thinking —
to feel the wet grass under my bare feet.

*The longed-for coolness after scorching sunshine. The freedom in my heart,
with nothing but rain, thunder, and storm around me. And a heart that was
still intact — feeling as strong as a hurricane.*

The world was mine alone. I fell in love with storms instead of
people. *And oh, what a blessing it was back then, when your heart belonged
to none other than yourself.*

I still run across meadows in my dreams — *screeching with laughter,
singing songs and wearing a smile as the most beautiful dress.*

Today I wonder when I stopped doing that.
And whether growing up comes overnight — or as a silent killer.

PEONIE'S NIGHTMARES

I stand in this endless field of rotting peonies. *Again.* Countless monochrome tones – the sky is a matt-white prophecy that almost blinds me. Ashes under my feet, soft as cotton. The smell of decay takes my breath away – *sweet and deadly* – a different kind of chloroform, *but oh, so lovely.* **Time. Stands. Still.** The silence fills all emptiness. *But not inside of me.* Not a single sound in the air. *No movement, no wind, no life.* I slowly feel the loneliness creep into my heart. The ashes rise to the sky like snow falling backwards. *Dust particles that sparkle in the fading light.* Even if I can't see through the dream state, I know what will happen next. *No demons,* I whisper. *Silence leaves my lips.* I look around; my red evening dress is the only color in all this gray. *No demons,* I repeat. *Not in this world.* And suddenly you stand there, inches but also miles away. You don't look at me and the panic starts to swallow my heart. I try to run towards you, *but I can't.* I'm stuck in the moment. I try to scream your name until my lungs burn *but I can't hear myself.*
I never reach you and I know it.

No demon could ever hurt me more
than you visiting my dreams
      — never noticing me.

TEMPORARY

"I knew someone like you is only temporary," she said. "I knew it from the very first word you said to me – *without a voice*. When you had no name and your appearance no contours. I heard the warning signs as they slowly scratched with their claws over metal but your soul was louder and your secrets too seductive. And because the darkness has always fascinated me, I threw myself into the abyss. Self-destruction has always been an art that I get lost in all too well. And I, the person who never trusts, trusted a stranger. I forgot myself – in every wonderful word you said. No matter how many times you promised we'd never lose each other, I was subconsciously waiting for you to vanish. I wrote metaphors for broken promises before you broke them. I wrote farewell letters before you were gone. Maybe that was why I missed you even in the moments when we shared secrets, cried and laughed together. I knew it all along. Like a premonition. Or a memory from another time. And when the day finally came, I broke anyway – *silently* – with an acceptance that shook me to the core. The aftershocks still echo through my soul. Maybe it wasn't your loss that broke me but the feelings I finally understood but never spoke out loud. And now I wonder if you knew."

HUNGER

Does the emptiness crawl
between the shadows
of your own darkness
to swallow every inch
of your fading light?

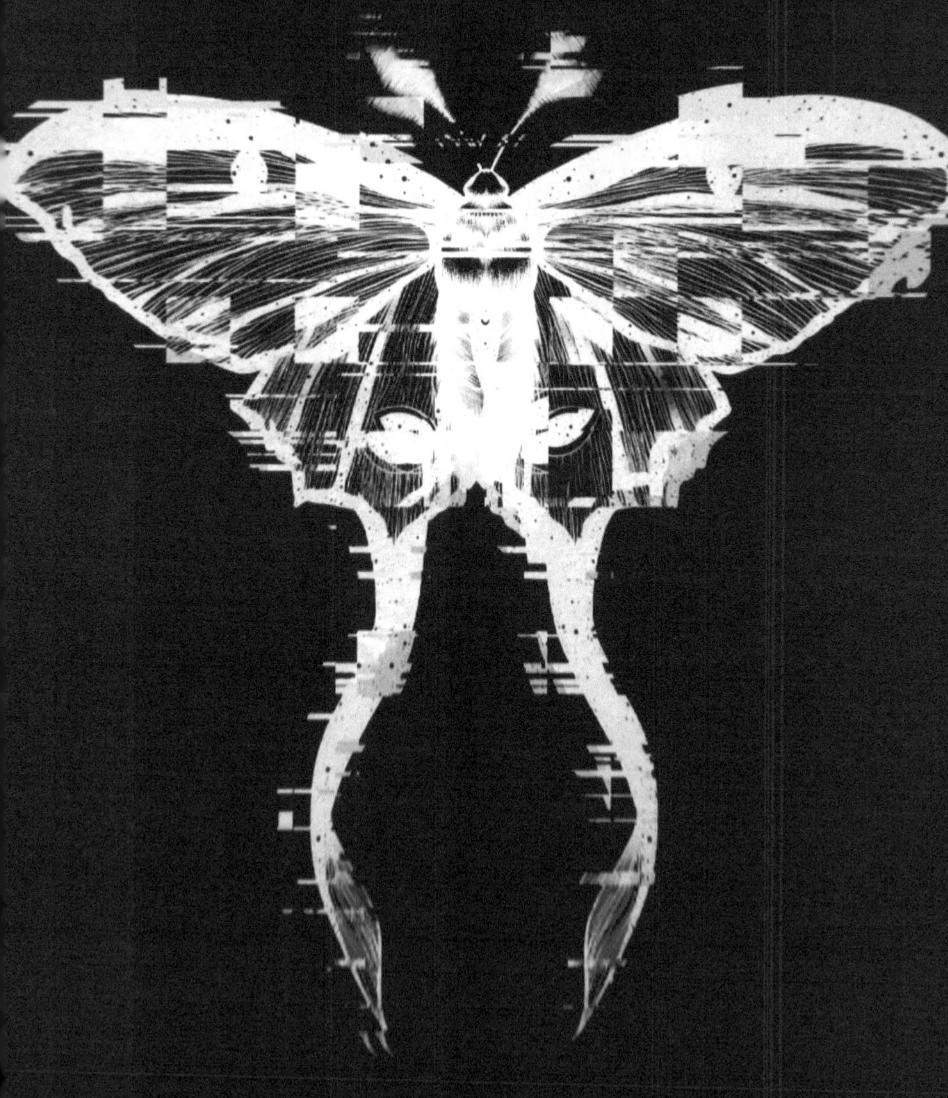

SOUL MATES

The ocean calls for me in a hundred voices,
but I never found yours.

Lie.

I *found.*

Magic.

Falling in love with someone else's soul
but knowing that you will never
belong to them feels
like drowning in
a starless
sea
.

THE SCENT OF SMOKE AND NIGHT

"I'll see you on the other side," he breathed, and his voice was the last thing that remained.

"Promised."

The room felt emptier than ever before.
She was crying even if she'd wake up any moment. Sobbing, she waited for the kiss of the real world. But something deep inside her knew that the hug would be painful and merciless.

Something is completely wrong ... Why do his words feel as sharp as knife-wounds, even though it was a promise?

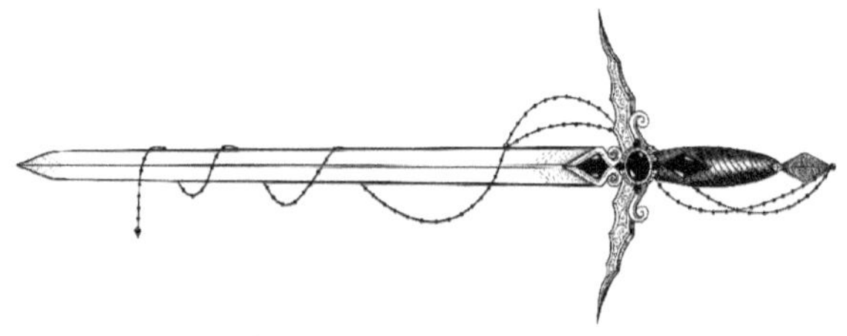

His lie hummed in her heart like a threatening melody until it finally tore her mind and heart apart.

It's so easy to tear someone's heart like paper.

And all that was left was the scent of smoke and night.

WARNING SIGNS

"I've found magic on a cold winter day and was instantly sure it won't stay long. I should not lose myself too deep in your dreams — or I'll break like the frost flowers under my feet."

A warning I wrote to myself after I met you.
It's a strange feeling when you know from the very beginning that things will end. That you only have time-limited moments. And even if you knew it from the depths of your bones – when the end comes, it crushes you with a weight that will leave you breathless for weeks.
Maybe you'll never recover.

The asphalt on that day was dark and sparkling – like you. You were a beautifully spoken promise. *Indispensable and deadly.*

Now I feel like this dream never existed.
I never existed.
You never
existed

Snow

"The silence feels so complete when it snows, don't you think?" he asked and his thoughts seemd far away. As if a part of him no longer belonged to this world.

You went home, right?, she thought. *To a place that only exists in your dreams. And I don't know if there's room enough for me.* "Yes, as if time would stand still," she answered instead. She stretched out her hand, watched the thick flakes melt as they touched her warm skin. "Like your memories," she whispered. *Like our magic. But that's the price, you know?*

He didn't seem to have heard her words, his eyes were so full of magic and emptiness at the same time.

"What are you thinking about?" she asked and reached for his hand – didn't dare to take it. Her fingers touched his, afraid of breaking the last remaining familiarity. *The air between us is so fragile. Snow in autumn is not that unusual.*

Before he answered, he closed his hand around hers. "Where we go, when we die."

These words took away any fear of closeness *but created a new one.* She put her head on his shoulder.

No one knows the answer.

Autumn is slowly being killed by winter's kiss and I wonder if you did the same to me.

3 AM

will slowly turn
into a memory
that only I
will remember

Déjà Vu

I feel the change like a flicker in the shadow.

A movement out of the corner of the eye
– just the invisible flapping of a moth's wings.

Almost imperceptible. stealingseconds.

And yet, it can trigger the end of everything. Moments fade with
every secret that is no more.

hasntthishappenedbefore?

Do you feel it too?

The nights flow through our fingers like fine-grained sand. We
move away from each other step by step, loosening the ribbon that
was tied around our souls. And now you're bleeding out the
memory of me, putting me aside like a discarded piece of clothing.
A skin that you've shed. Don't secrets lose their appeal when they
are revealed? *Ordinariness is nothing you can take.*

The moments we once shared
    fall around us like heavy rain
        but I think I've felt the drops on my skin
            long before the storm even began

MELODY

I am the quiet melody in your heart, whose notes are wrong, and you've forgotten how to use your own voice to sing it right.

I hope my echo reverberates through your soul.
I'll be the ghost who visits you in your lonely moments. When you walk down empty streets at midnight – I'll be the flickering neon lights reflecting on the wet asphalt. I'll be the name on your lips when no one's listening. I'll be the lullaby in the wind that whispers memories of moments that are long gone – *but never really forgotten.*

You may not recognize my voice every time, but you will feel my kiss on your lips when tears run down your cheeks
– *without knowing why.*

Maybe I was

        not strong enough

                to break your waves.

I.

Dear stranger,

another month has passed and still there's only silence between us.
To be honest, I wrote many letters – and especially this one I wrote so
many times I stopped counting. Sending this won't change a thing. But
I decided to do it because I've learned that in the end, you'll always
regret what you didn't speak out. And this is very important to me. I
promise I don't do it to harm or blame you, I do it to save myself.

FAREWELL

Do you remember the countless nights that were so lonely that you almost drowned in them?

I loved nothing more than to lose myself. *inallofyou. What did these nights mean to you?* Things change. *youdontevenmissmenow.* And while I smile, I break again. Time is a merciless killer. *And so is distance.* I shudder. Questions are singing through my mind but I'll never get answers. On days like these, I shake so badly that I feel like my bones are breaking. But I don't scream, *I miss you in silence. Ineedtoletyougo* in the way an addict has to let go their beloved drugs; all at once. *I need to tear every of your words from my bones. Untie every knot of the thread between us until the red webs fall like drops of blood. I don't care about the cuts they leave on my skin.* Because nothing hurts me more than waiting for you to miss me. The smoke and cinnamon scented wind gives me a feeling of magic that no longer lives in me. It strokes my skin like a distant memory. And I think of two things as I count the stars with tears in my eyes: Your lips always felt like magic. *And magic has always been just a bittersweet farewell kiss.*

thestrangerinmydreamswasneverinlove.

HOW MOON AND SUN BECAME STRANGERS

The nights are no longer the same
– like someone took their darkness away.
And oh, how much I fell for dark things.
I never belonged to daylight.
But you fell in love with the sun.

Let's meet in the shadows of twilight.

The truth is, I would have
run away with you anywhere.

– you just had to ask

COLLECTOR

I am a collector of words and memories.
Some things I'll banish on paper to make them immortal.
It's a blessing and a curse.

But I decide when I want to break again while reading those bittersweet lies

DROPS OF RUBY RED

The night is splintering cold
a scent of burned wood
floats through the air
mixed with the stranger's perfume
who walked in front of me for a while

I stop by the river
– fog hangs over the water
like spider webs, flying in the wind
my breath leaves my lungs
as white mist, while I look
at the starry sky

I've watched the same constellations
in the same place in August
when you said you missed me
before you fell asleep

One of the planets shines bright red today
– a sparkling drop of blood on obsidian

What an irony, I think,
as the stars melt into a
golden sea behind my tears

Like Paint on Your Fingers

Sometimes I wonder
when you made your decision
and how it was like to forget me

I imagined a lot of ways

Was it as easy as erasing
a line from your notebook?
Or more like locking the memory of me
in a box and bury it six feet under?

*I wonder if you thought just for one second about how I would feel or how much
I would cry or how many cracks my heart would get or if I'd even noticed what
you were trying to do with the knife you hid behind your lovely promises.
Oh, and they were all so lovely.*

I wonder if it was as tricky as washing paint
off your fingers that has already dried?
Or more like plucking off the crust of
an almost healed wound?

Did it even hurt a bit?

But darling, my soul has barbs
and my memory is like tar on your skin
You can try to wash it away
as often until your skin gets bloody

Better take steel wool

But the scent of me
will never leave your dreams

HUM

Your words hum inside of me like echoes in a burned-down cathedral. Nothing but remnants of times past. Isn't it wonderful to see me dancing in the ashes? Splinters of stained-glass windows under my feet. Glittering dust in the air. The crunch doesn't drown out your voice. And yet it's just silence you left — a hymn to my end. Still, I sing your name loudly in a hundred voices to forget that it was you who lit the fire — knowing that I'm still wandering through this dream.

RIVERS

We
flow
past each other
rivers of strangely
filled time
you replace
old memories
with new ones
like we never
really mattered
was I just
a void filler
or a cure
to your pain
I replace
my void
with poetic words
but the pain
flares under my skin
like a thousand
burning needles
You left nothing
but a feeling of
worthlessness
and a silence
that is louder
than thunder

.

WHAT IS YOUR TRUTH, DARLING?

Do you think

we stopped dreaming

because we felt

too much

or nothing

at all

?

— questions without answers

SOMEHOW

you broke me with such attention to detail
that I lost all my words.
I would forgive you anything.
But that my dear, outweighs everything else.

— Because what is a writer without their words?

51

DIAMONDS ARE A GIRL'S BEST FRIENDS

How could you
leave with all
these words
still hanging
in the air?

Like morbid
shimmering glitter
– obsidian
and ruby-red
as poisonous
as Belladonna

I breathe in
because I'd rather
choke on your residues
than to starve
on your absence

And I smile
in the most
beautiful way
as your crumbled
promises slowly
spread in my blood

But you don't even notice
the dying diamonds
in my winter-lake eyes

II.

This is my last letter to you.

I must do this because I can't take all this silence and ignorance any longer. It feels like all the things that happened last year, never really existed. Looking through our old messages is pretty destructive because it feels like all of this happened in another time or another reality. It's so fucking strange.

But your silence is the most honest answer I got from you. It broke me more than you can ever imagine. It hurt me so much that it changed me in some way. I've never felt so worthless.

Amnesia Kisses

You took away all of my beloved words
my lips tremble like I've forgotten
the lyrics of my favorite song
and that's the same as forgetting
everything that defines me

I feel like an illiterate
who stumbles over her own words
when I try to express the void you left
synonyms storming around
in my stomach like hungry moths

The eye of a hurricane
is nothing against your silence
beautifully whispered metaphors
have always been my greatest weakness
so, crash me with your deadly kisses
I have nothing left to lose

Except a story that was never mine

LIAR

The first snowflakes melt on my skin
and all I can think of
is the letter you promised
but never wrote

ONE DAY

And maybe the day will come
– months or years from now, when you'll stare at the night sky
searching for something you can't remember. But suddenly the
feeling of me will hit you like a brick wall.

Will you miss or hate me then?

DUCT TAPE

And maybe someday …
… I won't miss you anymore.

But until that day comes, I bravely breathe in rusty nails and try to hold my shattered heart together with duct tape.

My soul aches more than broken bones.

But there's something deeply poetic about binding invisible wounds, don't you think?

BUT WHAT IS LEFT OF YOU WHEN YOU
BROKE TO PIECES?

"What did he mean to you?"
"Too much. Losing him broke my ribs and changed everything
I was."

Sometimes the Things You Fear the Most Are Not the Monsters Under Your Bed

You fear me more
than your demons
that's why you
run
as far away
as you can
pretending that
I never existed

Elsie

"I think I'm cursed ..." she whispered. **"People always seem to forget me.** At first, it's starting with small things; like my favorite color, my favorite book, or where I come from. But that's not all. With every day it's getting worse. They forget the secrets they have told me, and the ones I told them. They forget the dreams we had, how we laughed and cried together. How I dried their tears. They even can't remember the color of my eyes. Or how I fought for their attention, without caring how much it hurt myself. No matter how close we were, at some point, they always started to forget. Something erases every memory from their mind – every feeling from their heart. And it makes me feel like I'm slowly dying – rotting like a flower because no one will ever miss or remember me. Not my face, not my words, not even my name. Like someone wants to take away all the people I love – *take them forever.*

I'll end like a ghost with no one remembering my story ..."

Sometimes
I ask myself
if feeling
too much
was worth
breaking
my neck
at the end
.

A Dream within a Dream within a …

Maybe
we were just a distant dream
created by an insomniac stranger
on a magic-kissed winter night
where he wandered
through so many worlds
in solitude

Our fate was sealed
as the first light of day
kissed his eyelids

GOODBYES PACKAGED AS COMPLIMENTS

Someone once told me that such a deep melancholy rested in my eyes, he'd fear to drown in the almost colorless blue.
As if my eyes were a mist-shrouded, dark forest in which you could hopelessly get lost.

And I didn't know what to answer.
Because I knew exactly that these words meant nothing but
... farewell.

Artist's Death

Let's crash like waves on cement.

— We never mattered anyway.

LIKE WE USED TO

The air smells so much like snow tonight — a perfume of winter farewells and cinnamon smoke. I listen to the silence while my breath freezes as it leaves my lungs. (I like the idea of frost flowers on my lips) I smile sadly as the memories of a long-forgotten century whisper through my mind — with an angel's voice so sweet, I would have cut my own throat if he'd tell me to. I wish we could return and start again, my wonderful demon. My forbidden love. I'd be your Persephone if you wanted me to. I'd be everything but daylight. Because my name means nothing but darkness, and in your hands, it's sparkling like the most beautiful nightsky. Now it's nothing but charcoal. I don't bare missing you another day. (Do you try to press diamonds by killing my heart?) Can we be strangers again? Let's forget our names and wander through dreams, like we used to.

To some people, you are only important as long as
they are lonely.

3 AM – PART II

What am I waiting for
3am
empty dreams
whispering your name
in a hundred voices
desperately hoping
for an answer

Where do my thoughts wander
3am
trembling hands
trying not to suffocate
on the nightmares
you breathed into my lungs

Where do my dreams go
3am
when I'm still wide awake
with no dream at all
only darkness on my skin
closer than you ever were

Where does my soul wander
3am
when the door is still hidden
and the key is still lost
in your memories
I break with every kiss
of daybreak's glance

Where does my heart float
3am
stuck in a stranger's dream
wandering through the ruins
of fading words and promises
trying to put the pieces together
well knowing, he's a riddle without solution

But I'm still here
3am
on the floor, bloody knees
staring into the eyes of a demon
but no one's staring back

16

I wrote 16 letters
knowing I would never send
one of them
I need to say goodbye to you
before it breaks me completely
but I would never go
without a single word
I could never be as cruel
as you were to me

At that time, I did not know that I would send one after all.

But I never got an answer.

.

We fade out like these once vivid dreams that now slowly turn into a land of ice and snow. I've tried to bury the memory of you but your eyes shine through the crystal like azure-blue rivers.

But the only thing I drown in
are empty promises.

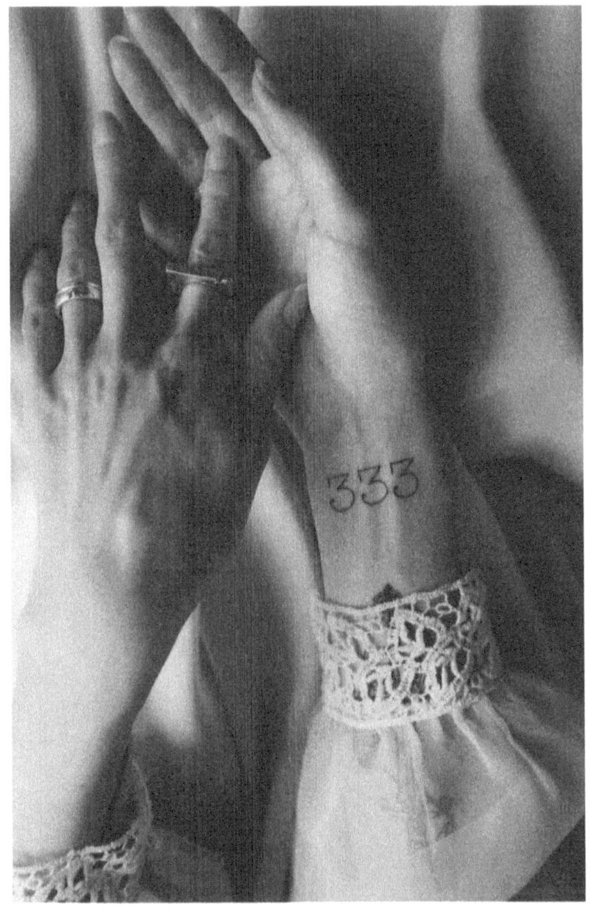

STARDUST

I still feel your presence – a fading aura flickering in the last light of the sinking sun.

Were you just a hallucination? Or a strange lucid dream? Or just a warning sign I ignored?

Soapbubblemoments.

Oh, how fragile we were.

My dear, how could we not shatter each other's hearts? The colors of our souls were too beautiful to last.

We were meant to end up as sparkling stardust.

Not All Sins Taste Like Honey

Now I swallow all the diamonds
and smile as blood runs down my chin
your name on my tongue tastes like metal
but you're still my favorite sin

We Were Never A Love Story

"Well ..." she said, head tilted to the skies, tears running down her cheeks but a smile on her lips. "Maybe we were just an accident the universe wanted to happen. But we crashed too hard to ever recover from it. That's the saddest thing, you know. To accept that our story was predetermined to end like this."

Run, Darling

Run as fast and as far away as you can.
If you think this is the only way to get rid of me, do it.

But remember one thing:

Running will never bring you salvation because no matter how far
the distance, you can never outrun your thoughts and heart.

There is a part of my heart that will always miss you. You've touched my soul with yours since the day we've talked for the first time. You became such a close friend of mine, and the distance never seemed important because you always felt so close. No matter how many thousand miles were between us. But now, the distance is growing like a hungry monster. And it's not because I want it but because you do. Nevertheless, I have to tell you that no matter what happens, no matter what ways you choose in your life, I will never forget you. Because I know that I've found what I've always been missing - what I was searching for in every night sky. I'm very grateful for that in a sad but heartwarming way. I think we helped each other, inspired each other and maybe also saved each other in some way. But maybe this connection always meant more to me than it did to you. Maybe I never meant anything at all. Sometimes I wonder if meeting you was worth the pain I have to feel now. And if I deserve the silence you punish me with. Yes, I know, saying that out loud is cruel. But then I remember how I used to feel when we talked back then and I realize, I could never unfeel that. You were the spark of magic that I need to let go now. And I genuinely hope with all my heart that you find all the happiness and love in the world. That someone will finally fill the void in your heart. Someone who understands you completely and is able to calm your demons. Because that's all you need.

PRIORITIES

You
never cared about
my demons

— So, I fought yours instead

I fell in love with the way you described your nightmares. So heavy and full of pain and with so much detail, it was easy to believe that you were really there when you were asleep.
Every time I tried to calm you down and accepted your fears as good as I could. I didn't bare the fact that the monsters would harm you, even in the real life. I would have climbed inside your dreams myself to kill the demons together with you.

HAUNT ME

Did you know you were the reason I started writing letters?
Now I'm sitting here, numb and with no idea why the hell I'm
writing this – it doesn't make any sense at all. Because no words –
no matter how poetic or how melancholy – can describe the pain
of how it feels like to be forgotten by you. Maybe you were just a
bittersweet melody that made my heart bloom under the softly
whispered stories of your deepest fears. And I have to confess,
even if I already said goodbye, I've never done it for good. How
could I ever forget the person I almost drowned in? (Isn't it funny
how I stumble from one goodbye to the next, and can never really
let you go?) All hope is gone. I didn't mean enough for you to fight
for this. You won't give me the answers I need so desperately to
save my soul. So, why do I keep you here? To still lie at myself that
everything is going to be okay in the end? Nothing is ever going to
be okay again. You left a mess of footprints in the snowy meadows
of my dreams. It's not as poetic as it sounds like. Friends don't
break each other's hearts. You chose. And your decision seemed as
easy as dropping a glass. But now, it's time for me to choose.
Ghosting time is finally over. Waiting for answers is over. Getting
hurt is over. If we should meet in another life, better leave it at
hello – before you take the chance to destroy me a second time.
Even if I'll miss you forever, it's okay. Everything is better than
waiting for a ghost that will never come back. Now it's my turn to
haunt your dreams.

DOORS

I opened my heart
to you completely
revealed you my deepest
feelings and thoughts

But you stayed silent
and chose to break
the last thing in my soul
that was not broken

Still, I try to find a way
back to you but you closed
every door and locked them
with the key I gave you

The Place Doesn't Matter

I bury your secrets in the snow.
    — white lies never looked so pretty.

I can lose myself in you like I lose myself in the sea.
But the sea has always let go of me. You drown me

— without touching.

Nameless

I got lost in you and I can't do anything about it. I dissolve like fog at dawn, and I don't know what will be left of me when it all disappears with you in another endless dream. I'm still here — formless like a ghost — only consisting of fragments of thought and shreds of memory.

— what happens to me if everyone else is forgetting my name?

NIGHTMARE

The monster is standing in front of my bed – *again*. A manifested darkness that soaks up all light around it. I stare at it and can't move. I recognize nothing but heavy shadows. *How can the color grey be so heavy?* The fear eats its way into my bones. I cannot breathe. The silence is all consuming. The monster is holding me down without touching me. I try to fight back every time but it's pointless.

My whole body is heavy as lead. I'm almost choking under the invisible weight that lies on my chest. I never manage to see through the dream state. I never manage to turn the light on. It never works. *Never.* And yet it seems to be my only goal. My screams collapse as if I'm under water. The monster just stands there and stares at me with its non-eyes. It never seems to end. *Dream in a dream in a ...*

It never ends ... Until I wake up bathed in sweat – still screaming. But this time my voice isn't silent.

What do you want from me?

You will always be
The most beautiful
Scar on my skin

Ruins

I was wrong about one thing:

I wasn't the writer – you are the best storyteller I've ever met.
Nobody has ever told me things that would never happen as
creatively and convincingly as you.
*You broke my dreams like one of your promises. And still, I wish you'd visit
these dreams again.*
Let's dance through the ruins ...
... and forget that the days never belonged to us dreamers.

NIGHTSHADE

Time has a strange consistency.
It changes its texture like clouds in the sky their shape. And with
each passing year, we feel the lost moments like merciless kisses
from nightshade.

Do You Know What I Miss?

The times when people still cared for each other. The times when we were young, and goodbyes weren't even on our minds. When friends were friends for years. The idea that things end sometime didn't exist for us. I miss the times when things lasted. Today it seems people only live for the moment. This world is full of superficial relationships and feelings. Time and bonds no longer have any permanence, no real meaning. People love fast, trust fast, hurt others easily and forget the ones who were important to them. You can do what you want and believe what you think is real – but it never really is. Because words are always just words in the end. Hollow letters without meaning. Because sooner or later they'll lose interest. They simply vanish. As if they were pressing a switch in their head to erase you as simple as a spot of dirt. They leave you collateral damages for a new, better adventure.

Most people live as collectors these days, regardless of how many empty ruins they leave behind.

Black Hole

Your abscence
left no void
it left a ghost
that can touch
and hurt me

My feelings for you
created a monster
that is haunting
my own dreams

2:07 AM

We met between the worlds
back then
before the days took you away
and turned me into a ghost
haunting my own nightmares
but I never really came back
from where you left me
I'm still there
in another reality
sitting next to you
above the roofs of the city
that only exists in my dreams
the world we created
out of words and promises
and magic
watching the stars
of a thousand dimensions
and I know
I'll love you through all of them
and I'll search for you
in every other life
until the memory of you
finally
stays

You cover my thoughts – *stream like black oil over my colors.* You erase all the words that I need for my memories, as if you wanted to prevent me from making you immortal. But no matter how much you etch yourself through my emptiness, I'll always find a way to capture you in words. *Bit by bit.* You are my personal demon that I fight with my own kind of magic. *Until one day, all your residues are gone from my heart.*

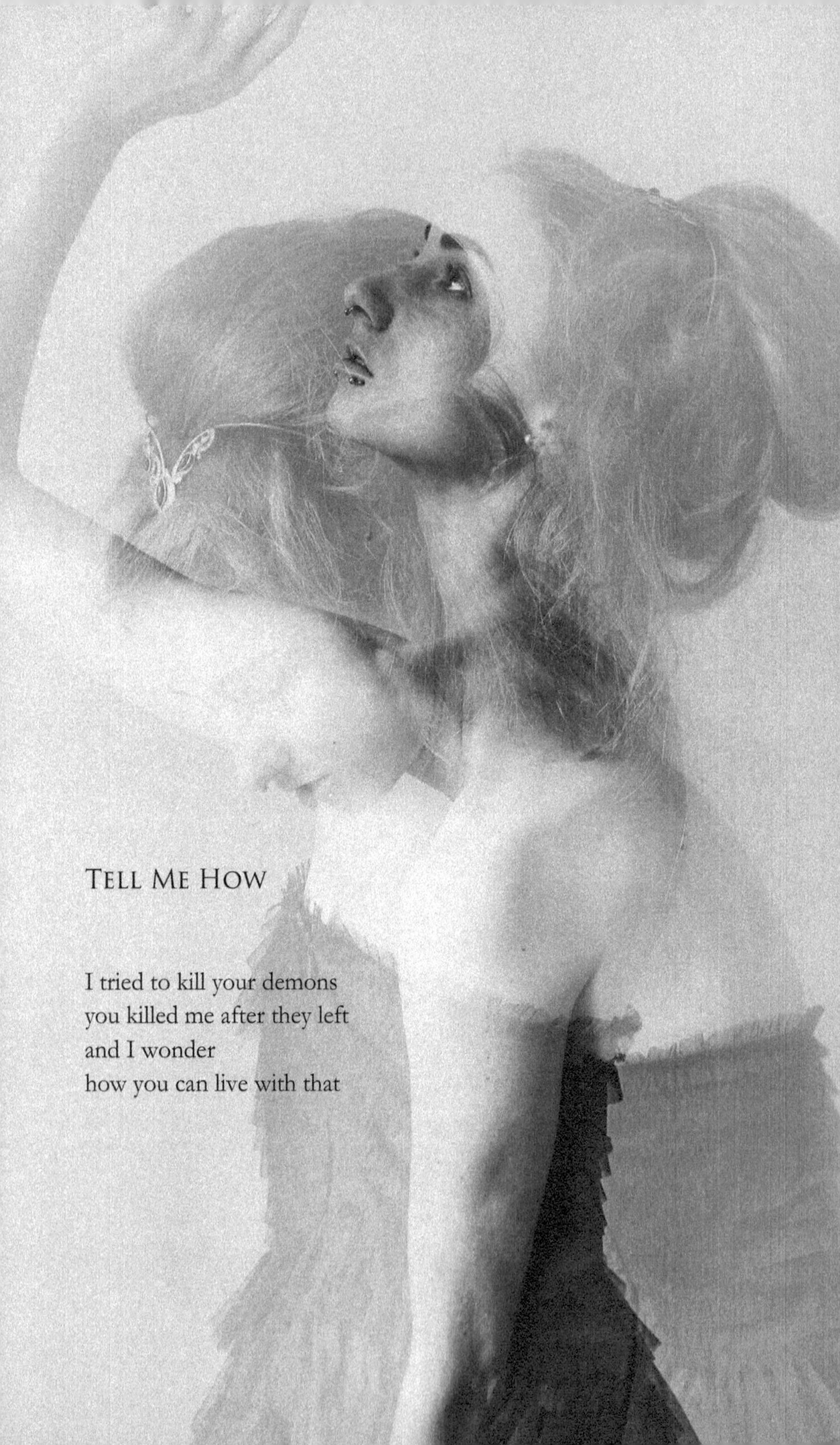

Tell Me How

I tried to kill your demons
you killed me after they left
and I wonder
how you can live with that

Give Unto Me

I miss the nights when you were drunk
and talked to me for hours without being afraid
of telling everything that was so heavy
on your shoulders for so many years

I still carry these secrets between my ribcage
and hope you're safe without them

I still remember the names of your demons

IV.

I hope you'll think of me sometimes, 3:33 am. That you proudly remember all the fights you have won in your nightmares. That I was always by your side and wanted to help you as much as I could. Your demons became mine too, and I wanted to kill them together with you. But hey, we did it, didn't we? Your insomnia is gone, and everything has changed. And maybe there will come a day ~ months or years from now, when you'll stare at the night sky ~ and maybe you'll remember ... You'll remember these long-gone conversations we had. All the things we shared. Maybe you'll remember the countless nights I stayed up just for you ~ listened to you, were there for you ~ when your demons haunted you. It wasn't just your war ~ it was mine too.

It seems like something's missing in my life since we don't talk anymore. A year ago, we met as strangers and now, end in the same way.

The Easy Way

You could simply save someone's life with a few words.

— But it's so much easier to step over the broken pieces instead of putting them back together, right?

Brush Stroke

You erased my name like I was nothing more than a misplaced brush stroke that you wanted to get rid of when you opened a new page in your book. In the end, words are nothing more than letters strung together. I was never important in your story.
My color was never waterproof.

And it was so incredibly easy for you to knock over a glass of water.

But it's okay.

I've learned how to get under your skin like permanent ink.

I Don't Want It Back

Sometimes I wonder
if all of this really happened
or if it was just a dream
I've lost my heart in

Last August

I remember that night
when shooting stars
were falling from the sky
like dying fireflies
sparks of magic lit up the darkness
while we were talking for hours

I never told you
I made three wishes for you
and they all came true
but the only thing
I wished for myself

didn't

.

BRANDED

I still remember what song I listened to
when the world around me
fell silent beneath the layers
of your words

I still know what the weather was like
and what I felt and how I wished
this moment would never fade
I collected so many details about you
that I could fill a whole book

I did

Then I remember
I've already written your story
long before we met

That's why I always knew
how bittersweet the end would be

and that it was not going to be
the end at all.

VISITOR

I can't say how many times I want to tell you about the things I do and how you are still in every piece of art I create. But you always knew what deep marks you have left on my soul, and I know that's the only way I can keep you close. And that makes me smile with tears in my eyes.

We leave marks on all the things we touch and lose. Fingerprints that can never be washed off again. No matter where we go
— we never go forever.

You left a mess of footprints in the snow-covered meadows of my dreams.
But you're still my favorite visitor,
because the worst chaos
always kept me calm

.

SPLINTER

And I wonder if you carefully planned to destroy me, or if it was a spontaneous experiment. Did you make me your personal work of art? Splintered souls glitter the most, am I right? And diamonds have always been your greatest weakness. But you didn't consider how sharp my splinters are.

— One day, one of them will reach your heart.

Ghost

I think you would rather fight the most dangerous demons a
hundred times instead of answering that letter, right? And I still
wonder what you are so afraid of ... or if I simply vanished out of
your memories because nothing was ever real.

– Oh, what a beautiful ghost you were

Braille

That's what happens when you touch a writer's heart.

I read the scars you left on my skin like Braille and create stories
from every splinter you left in my bones.

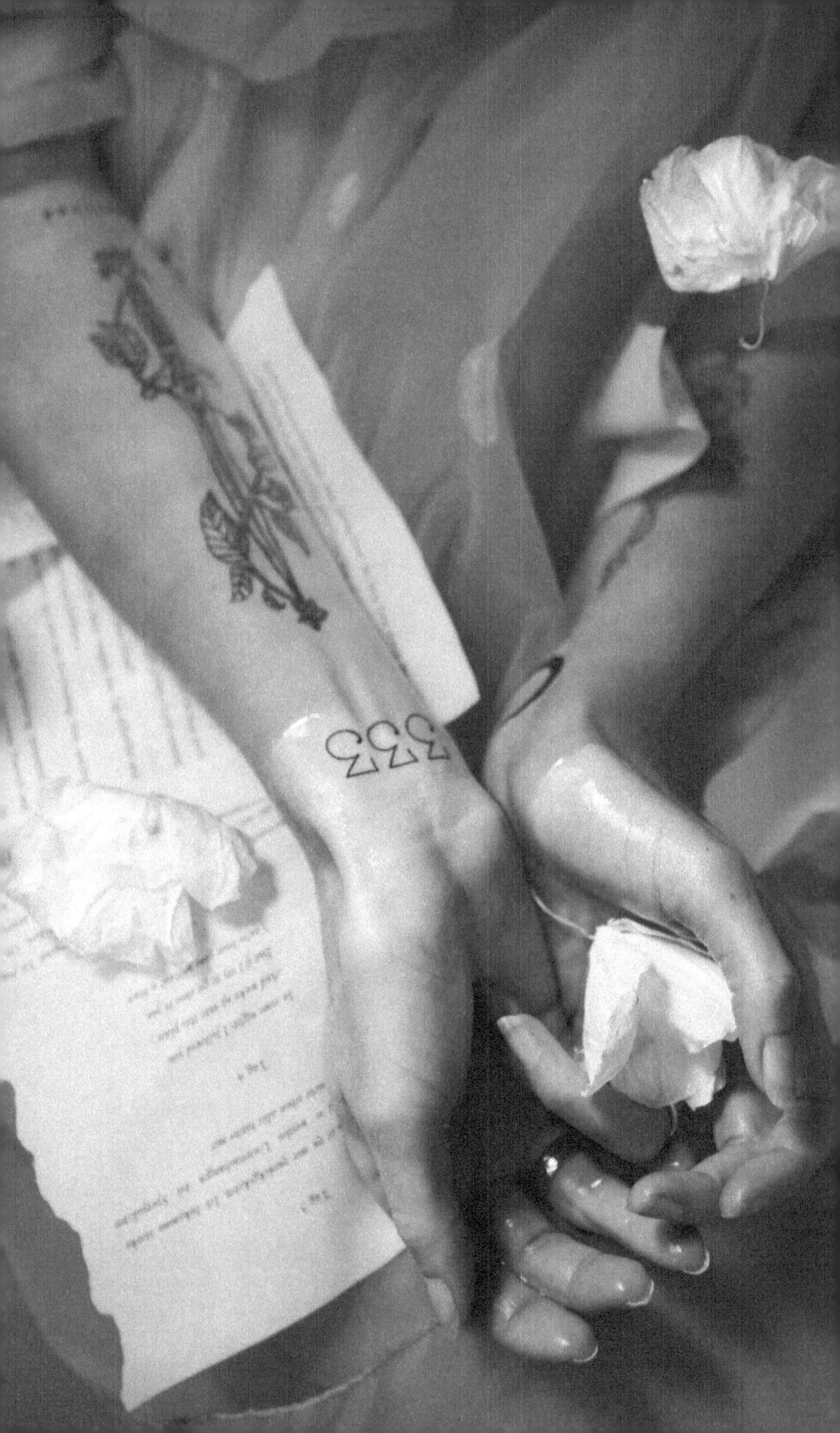

ABSINTH

You always had a strange way to write
– an artist that exactly knew how to burn holes in hearts and photographs in minds. I can still see the images rush past so clearly, as if they had been planted into my own memories. I close my eyes, listen to the song we both fell in love with and let the time-lapse run through my mind.

> *That night, the road was winding, moving like a snake. We flew with the current. Yellow line, rays of light. Worlds collide, we never touched. The darkness bloomed into monochrome shades of absinth. Invisible ghosts that watch the same film in different timelines — not meant to cross borders. The trees draw lines of surreal colors, melting time. Harsh contrasts reflecting forest spirits. Branches rushing by — dancing shadows. I listen to the melody in the background that lingers in the air like a hidden promise. Maybe you won't remember me. I feel ashes under my fingertips as I try to touch you. But it's me who turns to dust. You never really saw me.*

My darling, you have a black hole instead of a heart – you devour everyone who loves you.

> Your contours slowly dissolve ...
> *... and I with them.*

Choose Wisely

Someday
I'll be strong enough
to erase you the same way
you erased me
and when that happens
there's no way back
and your chance
to make things
right will be over

Time can be a murderer
so choose wisely

V.

I'm not expecting an answer. I don't want an apology. I don't want you to feel sorry for me. You don't have to explain yourself or find lies to do me a favor. And I'm sorry if I hurt you with my words but I don't regret voicing my feelings. I just needed to get rid of all of these words that were so heavy on my heart. I hope the weight will leave my shoulders along with this letter.

You should know I could never be angry or hate you that you no longer want me in your life. I'm just so incredibly sad, because I remember all of your wonderful words and every of your promises.

I still want the best for you. My image of you will never change. You were one of my greatest inspirations and one of the most wonderful humans I've ever met. I will never forget all these strange coincidences that happened to us – for me it was a spark of magic in this far from perfect world. I'll never forget the countless times we talked for hours. The deep thoughts we shared but also the funny times you made me laugh so much. You were truly a great friend with a beautiful soul – You understood me like no one else. That's why losing you tears me apart now. I thought connections like these would last for a lifetime but some dreams are just hopes and fairy dust – they burn far too easily.

Perhaps, I will never know what lit the match.

I will keep the memory of you in my dreams.

Goodbye, my dear.

GAMES

You
my dear
have taught me
a different level of pain

Many Ways

Sometimes I just stroll lethargic through my own labyrinth. Like I've lost something but know for sure I won't find it here. Still, I can't stop searching. And I still can't forget the things I shouldn't think about.

The "why" haunts me like a mantra every single day. But it seems like it isn't even worth sacrificing a few minutes of your life to take the burden of uncertainty off my shoulders.

I've thought about it for so many hours and days. I've walked hundreds of ways in my head but never reached the exit. I'm stuck in a dead end and you're building one wall after the other.

The first and cruel way: *You were never the person I thought you were and it's no problem for you to throw people away like garbage if you don't need them anymore.*
Second: *You are afraid of your own truth.*

I wish for the third but that's a secret I hold closer than you hold your silence.

MOONLIGHT LIES

I did not notice
how the night drew near

Something mixed in
like an invisible poison
that changed me for you

Did I become your most feared demon?

I miss the nights in which
we scattered feelings like moon dust
when you still missed me
and I was still whole

I forgot I never was

Overcoming distances
was never your intention
your daylight promises
turned into midnight lies
and now I can never stop
to scatter, to fade, to dissolve

Broken things sparkle the most

I once thought worlds of you
now everything I thought you were
is buried under ruins

EMPTY TRAINS

I hope
You still think of me
for a few seconds
when you sit
on an empty train

Sunlight on your skin
while you wish for snow

I hope you'll smile
without knowing why
and I'll smile too
in another world
always remembering

IMPACT

We collided a long time ago.

Still, I can feel the earthquakes shaking my bones. The cracks run
through me like rivers in the dark.

— Oh, darling, you left a bottomless abyss inside of my heart

SILVER

The darkness shatters.

And as I look at the constellations, I shatter on the memory of you.
The night sky seems to explode into millions of silver sparkles
behind my tears. I could name them a hundred different colors.

But of what use would it be? You are color-blind, Darling.
For you, I have always been just the black between the silver.

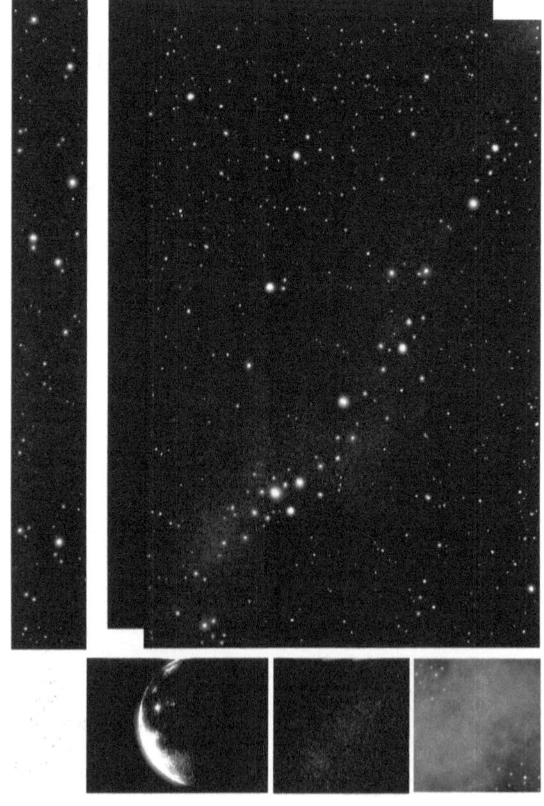

STARRY

Maybe I've found what I've always missed – what I've been looking for in every night sky.

I don't know which feeling is crueller – knowing that you have lied to me with a passion that makes me shudder, or that I will never see the stars in your world again.

– Your darkness shatters the stars, darling.

Magnolia's Lullaby

The sky is almost
white today
a kind of dusty gray
with a hint of sunlight
wistfully reaching
through the mist

Snowflakes are falling
in slow motion
sparkling white petals
kissing pink magnolias
with deadly softness

“Maybe I am awake in your dream.”
“Maybe you are.”

You are no more, darling
maybe you never were
but I'm still in love
with the idea
of you

.

The void you left turned into a freezing acceptance that runs through my soul like cracks on a winter lake. Your silence is screaming in my head like a thunderstorm rushing through the halls of a cathedral. I miss your voice in a way I would miss the stars if I'd never see them again. I miss the taste of the words you breathed into my lungs without ever touching my lips. But now, the pain has reached a dull numbness that I can almost bear. As if I were under water – looking at the world through a cloudy jar filled with cotton wool.

I.

Miss.

You.

If I had to give melancholy a color, I would name your eyes. You have always been beautiful to me – the way forbidden and broken things are beautiful. To me, you are like blood on snow or the inky berries of a belladonna. You told your lies with such a deadly softness – *sweeter than burned sugar could ever taste* – I would lick them from your lips anyway.

Your demons will never leave my dreams.

But maybe you still see me, 3:33 am – remembering that I will always be awake in your dream – so no demon can ever harm you again.

STRANGER'S SONG

Sleep well, my thief of words. Sleep deeply and dreamlessly. Maybe we'll meet again – *3:33 am* – when your heart beats in another world. Reminding you that I'm still awake in your dreams – fighting your demons, so you never have to be afraid again.

ROSE GARDEN

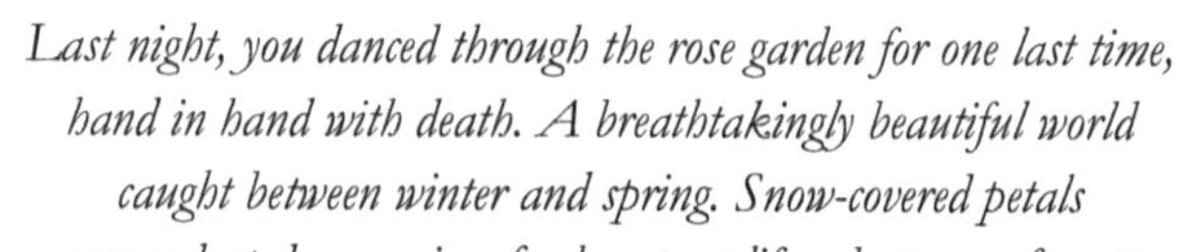

Last night, you danced through the rose garden for one last time,
hand in hand with death. A breathtakingly beautiful world
caught between winter and spring. Snow-covered petals
– sugar dusted memories of a long past life – but never forgotten.
So, rest now, in the softest embrace
of a thousand flowers
– and dream.

WHISPER

I have always kept my feelings for you as a secret.
Because I learned one thing:

— You never tell a dream walker that you are in love.

The air smells of rain and tobacco
and the pain I feel, almost makes my lungs collapse.

You've started to forget about me
and there's nothing I can do.

122

I CAN'T ESCAPE YOU.

[333] I'm still chasing answers
in a labyrinth I created myself

– but you were never there.

You

were

never

here

PASTEL

We crashed a long time ago but I still feel the earthquakes in my bones. Would the truth burst my flesh open, even if you'd whisper it to me in the same sweet voice, you used to tell your pastel lies?

ARTIFACT

The pain you caused
is kind of gone
and left nothing but
a starless void
between my ribcage

*Oh, what wonderful names I could give
all that various shades of black*

I don't even remember
the feeling you gave me
or what it was like
to share all these secrets
with a stranger

*Who forgot me, with every demon
he left on my shoulders*

The only remains
that make me realize you existed
are a few quotes in my notebook
and an artifact I wear like a dagger
to remind me every day
that I survived you

*And as I write this down
I feel like a sleepwalker, forgetting the only dream
I ever really wanted to get lost in*

Nyctophobia

I remember
how you told me
you only dream
in monochrome

Colors never were your thing

So I painted
your nights
in liquid gold

But light was never what you wanted

Your demons
went up in flames
and I, with them

Diamonds

The snowflakes glitter like diamonds in the sun.
I remember you saying, you wanted to meet me one day in winter.

— I'll never stop waiting because I can't accept that it was all just a lie.

Maybe a dream, but not a lie.

Moon Struck

I want to kiss the
moonlight
from your lips
and taste your
nightmares
on my tongue
I swear I'd never
thought
your demons
would taste
like cinnamon

INK

I wonder
if I am the only one who suffers
and if the pain of missing you will ever stop
can you please tell me the secret of
how you overwrote the memory of me
so easily, like spilling a jar of ink
on every word we ever shared?

I can't stand the fact
that I'm not worth remembering

Storm

You were fickle like the weather, darling, although you wanted to be my solid rock. Remember how you said, you hoped we would meet in the next life too, if this one is not enough? And yet, here I sit – in the shards of your words.

> Wondering if maybe you were never the stable rock
> – but simply the object that I broke on.

If we could change the constellations
with just a few written words,
what would have happened
if our lips *almost* touched?

HUSH

Sometimes I wonder how you could trust me with all these secrets,
all these stories and feelings, only to disappear silently, leaving not a
single answer behind.

— the boy with the golden words fell silent like his own nightmares

"It's winter where he is now. I can't reach him. No matter how close we were – we've never been further apart than we are now."

"Different timelines – I am awake when he's asleep. But it's worse than that. The distance between us has grown like a hungry monster. We'll never be able to be close again, even if we wanted to."

"What's your name?"
"Does that matter? You'll forget it anyway."

In Pieces

Maybe now
I'm just another artifact
in your collection of
sparkling shards

Oh, do I look pretty enough for you in pieces?
Dusty memories hold your rotten heart together

Maybe sometimes
you open the box
just to watch how my blood
sparkles on your fingertips

You can't cut my voice
out of your mind

Maybe forever
I'll be the stranger
in your dreams
whispering the three words
that bring you to your
knees

VOID

I wonder if you still think of me sometimes
or if I am erased from your memories completely.

*But wouldn't "completely" mean that I am no longer the same as
before because a part of me no longer exists?*

And nothing could describe the void in my soul
better than that.

YOU

As I look up at the starry sky – *the air too warm to fall asleep* – I fragment my feelings into tiny little pieces.

A quiet thunderstorm is raging on the left side of the sky, and it feels like I'm not really here. *Or the thunderstorm isn't really here, who knows?* It's completely quiet – no thunder, no wind. Only lightning shines through the already moonlit night. Lost in thought, yesterday's firefly comes to visit me again, as if it wanted to remind me of reality. I thought fireflies were long gone and this was just the vague ghost of a nostalgic memory.

But does a ghost visit you a second time?

I am so mesmerized by the moonlit clouds and the little star that shines on my hand that I can no longer tell whether the stars are moving or standing still between the gaps in the pitch-black sea.

Are the clouds just fluorescent monsters?

And I wonder if this is still the same sky under which you told me last summer that I am the last thought on your mind before you fall asleep. *I doubt* – the stars and reality. The voice that comes out of my headphones sings about fireflies and goodbyes. I have to think of the shooting star you told me about back then and how I asked you to make a wish because that's the law. I smile.

Crack in time.

The sky is no longer the same when suddenly a shooting star flashes between a hole in the clouds. Collapsing realities.

My realities are collapsing more and more, I think.

I hear your promises shatter even across worlds – a lullaby you wrote for my end but never sang with your own voice.

Then I break and cry out of my soul what the thunderstorm doesn't do. I wait until the song ends the memory of you. But instead of redeeming me, I am drowning in a wave of unanswered questions.

I planned to stop believing in magic but nights like these make it incredibly difficult for me.

PROMISES ARE JUST LIES POSTPONED

You have your peace now but what about me?
Instead of making things right you burned everything down and
left more questions than answers.

*— Your promises always had the same value as the ashes and blood sticking on
your fingers*

I DON'T THINK YOU EVER REALIZED I WAS REAL.

I was just a distant dream – *a ghost for who you've had some strange feelings,* because it's easy to fall for an idea you were able to create yourself. Maybe you found out what I feel for you and that made me way *too* real. *Terrifyingly real.* And because you already have so many ghosts haunting you, you decided to run instead. *You feared nothing more than this connection becoming more real than your nightmares.* You were strong enough to fight the demons in your dreams – but you couldn't fight me.

– Because I am the only ghost you ever fell in love with

Do You Even Remember My Name?

Missing you feels like walking down an empty street at 4 am, not remembering where I'm going.

– a sleepwalker who got lost in a stranger's worn-out dream

UNTANGLE

I break the connection and cut myself hundreds of times on the rusty wire of your promises. I untangle dream by dream with bloody fingertips. Thread by thread, I loosen your words, even though I almost lose myself with every letter. Knot by knot, I unravel our fate until we become exactly as what we have started.

– Strangers.

But you know what?
I never completely make it. The last thread sticks to my heart like tar.

– one last glowing spark of hope

9:34 P.M.

The sky sends its next downpour.
It's almost dark and my eyes get lost in the dense
ink-blue. Last year at the same time, we were as
close as we could ever be, across worlds. My eyes
get cloudy. I miss your voice but I know I will
never hear it again. My thoughts grow cold like the
asphalt on which the rain hits.

CHANGE

This summer doesn't feel like summer.
I'm not sure why but it's like I'm waiting every day for that carefree feeling to come – *but it doesn't come*. And the days go by and nothing happens. The sand in the hourglass is emptying and the emptiness fills me. I don't know what has changed, or whether it's just me who's changing. Perhaps the feeling of endless summers you experienced as a child is now nothing more than a nostalgic memory. Nostalgia always feels more beautiful than the moment itself. I really wish I could still be naive enough to feel this magic.

Last summer was somehow different.
I miss things. Some absences changed me.

The magic is gone, and I'll have to find a way to live without it.

Drowning In Air

Sometimes your absence is literally choking me. I drown in the words that memories are whispering in the silence of some fragile moments – when I feel so lonely in all of my pain. I miss the way you understood me with such a clarity, as if we were breathing the same words and feelings.

– I think the universe will never forgive us for breaking this bond

New Demons

I wish I had been worth the kind of goodbye to you that would
have outlasted whole worlds. Instead of answers, you left me in
deafening silence. *All is quiet,* you think. But you're oh, oh so
wrong. I still remember the names of your demons.

— You made me one of them.

I will sing you the sweetest lullabies.
I will paint you the most beautiful nightmares.
I will crawl under your skin and stay there forever like permanent
ink.

— I've never felt more like a ghost than I do now

Maybe I'll make friends with your old demons.

And we'll haunt you.

BLURR

I miss the time when the nights were ours and reality blurred into something different under the power of our thoughts. I miss how your words merged into silver liquid, covering my heart in moonlight glimmer. I miss how it felt when our secrets intertwined and became such a strong bond that – after all this time – I can still feel the remnants of the rusty threads plucking at my heart. I miss the way you understood me with such familiar clarity as if I were made of crystal – which you never really touched because you were too afraid that your own truth would shatter. I miss the stars calling my name and what it was like to feel the magic in every word you said. And now I wonder – broken as never before – if I am the only one who still remembers.

Golden

The smell of burnt cinnamon
hangs in the air
an unfulfilled promise
breathes over my lips

I feel you between
my heartbeats
under my skin

I shudder wistfully
as the magic
ties new threads
after such a long time
in secret

Falling shooting stars
your silent gift to me
chasing away ghosts
weaving new promises

But before I can whisper
your name you are gone
but it's okay, I will wait
because darling, time
has no meaning for us

And I smile
while the world
drowns in golden stars

PERSEID NIGHTS

Tonight, the stars are falling
– glowing sparks on charcoal.
My memory becomes clear when I think
of last year's Perseids. At that time,
luminous promises were made. Now the
ashes of burnt wishes stick to my
hands. Bittersweet nostalgia overwhelms
me. *I close my eyes, summer nights. We
talked for hours.* I can still see the
image of your demon clearly. The first
shooting star fell, and you revealed me
its name at the same time. And the
first thing I had wished was that you
would be strong enough to defeat them.
Every shooting star – *the same wish.*

I smile because I know how it ended.
I had only one wish for myself. *But I
have always kept it a secret, my lovely
dream walker.*

Until one day, you might ask.

HEY YOU,

I know I probably don't cross your mind much anymore, but you still cross mine.

I wonder how you're doing and if you're happy with your life right now. I often think about what kind of person you have become and whether I would even recognize the new you. I guess not. But hopefully some little details may never change. I smile because I still remember the way you drink your coffee and what your favorite number is. In some moments, I wish I could give back all the left-over information I have of you, but they're too tangled in my memories. (It seems you used steel wire to fix them, didn't you?) Sometimes it's hard because the memories always fall on me when I don't expect it. I can't listen to *Fourth of July* without earthquakes shaking my bones. But I listen to it anyway. *Hey you.* Can you hear my voice whisper when you sit alone on a train? Maybe the passing clouds remind you of moments long gone. *Snowflakes on your windowsill. The names of your demons. Shooting stars. Hey you.* I wonder if you still have the letter I sent you a year ago, or if you've burnt it with every thread of our connection. I'm still wearing the artifact I got from you in another reality, because it's the only proof you really existed. (And I'll take it with me into the next life.) *Hey you.* Life is strange, isn't it? Time is rushing by, even though it feels like yesterday when you promised me to cherish this connection for a lifetime. Maybe we always had a different view of what that meant. *Hey you.* I know you're a different person now and I hope it made you a happier person, too. I hope it still works to banish your demons behind the door I created for you. I still care for you and pray that you're fine. Even though I wish the boy with the nightmares would still live inside of you because I miss him like hell. (I know it's wrong to drown in nostalgia, but I do that sometimes.) *Hey you.* When you look at the starry sky, who do you think of? I wonder if you ever understood the meaning of that one last poem and if that was the reason why you fell silent all at once. *Hey you.* I hope you knew what you have meant to me and how losing you tore me apart. I wonder if you ever wrote a reply to my letter or if you just never sent it. I pray that you'll do, one day. And until that happens, we will remain what you made us again.

    – *Strangers.*

ACKNOWLEDGMENTS

Some encounters hit us with such force that they leave something behind in our hearts and change us irrevocably. Scars as deep as abysses. You were the strangest feeling that I have ever felt. You were so much and nothing at the same time. I wrote poems about being forgotten and what it feels like to transform into a ghost. I wrote 16 letters that I never sent – except for one. Maybe it's hidden between these pages – defragmented into poems. I cried words for the answers I never got.

This is a story about magic and its price.
This book is about how I found and lost you
and the metamorphosis in between.

About the Author

Melanie Strohmaier is an author from Germany.
She loves icy winter nights and lonely walks in the dark – but also endless summers and starry night skies. She always tried to find words for this longing in her chest. Now her poetry books are the result of countless daydreams and sleepless nights. Maybe she found what she was searching for in her dreams but couldn't keep it.

Her published books:

Hannahs Traum (2019) - Selfpublishing
Der Traumwandler - Arkanas Ruf (2020) SadWolf Verlag
Awake In Your Dream - 333 (2020) - Selfpublishing
Der Traumwandler II - Der Fall des Monsters (2021) - SadWolf Verlag

belladonnasdream.com
www.instagram.com/melaniestrohmaier.autorin
www.instagram.com/herzstillstand
e-mail: melanie@strohmaier.com.de

VI.

After thousands of dead ends that I crashed into in my labyrinth of "what if's", I finally may have found some kind of peace. Even if I never reached the exit, I now know, that maybe the answer wasn't the solution at all. I thought I had to decipher the "why" to save myself, so I was desperately waiting for your absolution. I was sure I needed to hear it from you to keep me from falling apart. That it wasn't me who destroyed everything. I've searched in every corner of my being just to find the blame on myself. In all the pain that was driving me crazy, I came to the conclusion that all of this may have been a lie. That none of what happened was real. That every promise you made was because you wanted it to break – to break me. That it never meant anything that I went into battle with you to kill your demons. I even turned the beautiful moments into illusions. But now I know, you didn't destroy me – I did it myself. And whatever your reasons were, maybe you had to do it. Maybe there was no other way out for you, and you never meant to hurt me. Maybe this time you weren't strong enough to save someone else instead of yourself. It's all okay. You have always been pure magic to me, and I will keep you in my heart as just that – a strange and wonderful dream.

I will hold onto the beautiful moments. Because this way, I can never really lose you. You are everywhere – in the starry sky – in the cold winter air – in the scent of earth after a thunderstorm. You are in every word, in every sentence, in every one of my stories. I intertwine memories and make you immortal. And somehow, that makes me happy – in all my sadness. Maybe you can feel the same for me too. I forgive you and maybe we'll meet again, one day. Not in this life but in another world – 3:33 am – when everyone is asleep and I'm wide awake. Because this is the place where I can always feel you. I wait for you there.

See you soon, dreamwalker.

They say you always meet twice in life.

Next time I'll be prepared.

333